V4Y

VICTORY4 YOUTH!

7 Keys to Succeeding Against the Odds

OTIS WILLIAMS

Foreword by Les Brown

Praise for *VICTORY 4 Youth!*
7 Keys to Succeeding Against the Odds

This workbook is a **"VICTORY 4 Youth."** In today's society, many of our young people are without good solid role models from which they can learn values. This workbook fills in the gaps between the role model's influence and the ability of the youth to integrate the values they deem important into their personality. By systematically letting the youth work with all aspects of each topic covered, they come away with an intimate understanding of terms that are only too often thrown at them by people who themselves have no idea what they mean. I highly recommend this workbook not only for young people, but for all who want to refine themselves.

—David Weis, AmeriCorps Member,
American Youth Foundation—St. Louis Partners AmeriCorps

"VICTORY 4 Youth! is a step-by-step manual for those young people who are serious about making changes in their lives. Given the critical problems in today's society, it is imperative that we encourage our youth to begin the process outlined by Otis. The stories are inspirational; the lessons, instructional. The consequences of <u>not</u> pushing our youth toward **V-I-C-T-O-R-Y** will be to our collective detriment."

—Kimya M. Moyo, Founder/Director, SANKOFA Educational Program,
Teacher, School for Creative & Performing Arts, Cincinnati Public Schools,
Former National Recipient of The National Council of Negro Women, Inc.
Excellence In Teaching Award

"What are educators, employers, police officers, and community leaders desperately seeking in America's youth? Character—the self-respect, confidence and discipline required to be successful in our society. *VICTORY 4 Youth!* is a practical workbook that can give young people and their mentors a process and the tools needed to succeed today and tomorrow, against the odds."

—Lee Reading, Executive Director
Joy Outdoor Education Center

"Otis Williams continues to offer motivation and useful resources to help individuals set achievable goals through his workbook—*VICTORY 4 Youth!* In this book concrete steps are presented along with concepts that also emphasize values that today's youth should implement into their daily living. *VICTORY 4 Youth!* is a *"must"* for all."

—Leslie S. Kreines, Chairperson
Hamilton County Youth Conference

"*VICTORY 4 Youth!* is a very practical workbook that will help persons of all ages better set goals and plan for success. The biographical sketches are powerful testaments of persons succeeding against the odds."

—John Bryant, Executive Director
Cincinnati Youth Collaborative

"*VICTORY 4 Youth!* needs to be incorporated into every high school curriculum. It is an essential course for equipping our youth with the vitally fundamental knowledge and skills necessary for a bright future!"

—Mary A. Dobbins,
Single, career mother

"The most important thing about goals is having one! *VICTORY 4 Youth!* is very motivational and encouraging for high school students. This book helps develop wisdom and character for students by creative hands- on experience."

—Dr. Lionel H. Brown, Deputy Superintendent
Cincinnati Public Schools

"WOW! What a powerful tool. *VICTORY 4 Youth!* will play a major role in changing people's lives. The information included in this workbook will help teenagers with a step-by-step program for getting through the tough times. Every teenager should have a copy of *VICTORY 4 Youth!* to help them plot the course they need to become the best they can be."

—Rick L. Metzger, Professional Speaker and
Former World Cup of Powerlifting Gold Medallist

"Every young person has the potential to make a difference. In his book, *VICTORY 4 Youth!*, Otis Williams brings to life the essence of success with practical lessons which every reader can and will use."

—Dick Aft, President
United Way & Community Chest

"*VICTORY 4 Youth!* is one of those practical, makes-sense resources that can help guide young people in the right direction. It certainly will help young people gain insight into what really makes them tick!"

—Roger C. Effron, Retired Cincinnati Public School Principal
and Otis Williams' Principal at Aiken High School

"*VICTORY 4 Youth!* is a practical and highly useful guide to achieving one's full potential with many excellent exercises for self-reflection that I believe readers will find of real value."

—John E. Pepper, Chairman of the Board and Chief Executive
The Procter and Gamble Company

"*VICTORY 4 Youth!* can be the key to opening the door to a positive future for our youth. 'Opportunity knocks'—open the first page and enter the road to success."
—Greg Love, Vice President
YMCA of Metropolitan Dayton

"Otis Williams has demonstrated once again that he is the man for the hour. *VICTORY 4 Youth!* is what every young person needs to ensure success."

—Rev. Damon Lynch, Jr.
Pastor, New Jerusalem Baptist Church
President, Baptist Ministers Conference

"Otis has the power to inspire and help guide the young adults of today's troubled society. He brings out l imitless thoughts and helpful strategies to make the lives of the youth easier and less troublesome. This book can enlighten a person of any age."

—Doug Hall, Founder and CEO
Richard Saunders International and
author of *Jump Start Your Brain*

"*VICTORY 4 Youth!* succeeds in that it doesn't "tell" young adults what to do. Instead it offers a path, an opportunity for them to set personal goals and then make them reality."

—Patrick S. O'Brien
Author of *Making College Count*

"*VICTORY 4 Youth!* presents a refreshing approach to working with young people. It is process-oriented and highly engaging. Most significantly, it encourages individuals to examine their own value systems. In addition, it provides young people with the knowledge that they have options; they have the right to make informed decisions as they move through adolescence. In an age where too much of the emphasis in health education is merely on the delivery of information (facts), this book pushes kids to a higher level, a struggle with contemporary moral issues. The emphasis is on application, not just information."

—Thomas B. Main, Head of Upper School
Cincinnati Country Day School

"Otis Williams has taken the meaning of the word *VICTORY* to a higher level in this powerful hands-on guide for our youth. It contains the key ingredients, solutions, and support for youth to overcome the challenges they face on a daily basis."

—Sheila J. Adams, President and CEO
Urban League of Greater Cincinnati

"Being a high school student I see, first hand, young people who really want to be successful but struggle to find motivation or just don't know where to begin. *VICTORY 4 Youth!* is just that starting point for the young person who is determined to succeed and willing to make the commitment to do whatever it takes to reach positive goals."

—Daniel Miree, Jr., Senior
Winton Woods High School

V4Y

VICTORY4 YOUTH!

7 Keys to Succeeding Against the Odds

OTIS WILLIAMS

Foreword by Les Brown

TABLE OF CONTENTS

DEDICATION

This book is dedicated to my mother, Sarah Mae Smith, whose example showed me that the only limits are the ones I put on myself.

Thanks Mama—I love you!

FOREWORD

Few will disagree that the pressures facing our young people today are greater than in any previous generation. The soaring drug abuse, school dropout, teen suicide, and youth violence rates indicate that far too many young people are ill equipped to handle the day-to-day challenges in their lives.

Parents and educators who have used the *VICTORY 4 Youth!* Action Planner agree that it gives today's young people a fighting chance to make it through life—not as victims of negative influences, but as responsible young adults leading lives of purpose and integrity. Scripture reminds us "People *without* vision perish" while "People *with* vision prosper"—becoming assets to their communities rather than liabilities. The *VICTORY 4 Youth!* Action Planner will help teens make the right choices that will guide them to lead productive adult lives.

Its methods and techniques will help our young people govern their behavior with values, based on integrity that empowers them to have the courage to resist negative peer pressure. The worksheets teach our youth critical thinking skills that will be crucial to their success in a knowledge-driven world.

The author of this much needed life manual, Otis Williams, speaks and writes in a style that connects and impacts today's youth who are desperately looking for direction. I know first hand Otis does not just talk the talk—**"He walks the walk." "He is the message that he brings."**

The *VICTORY 4 Youth!* Action Planner will inspire our youth to create opportunities where there are none. They will learn how to take responsibility for their own destiny. After using and applying these success principles, they will become self-driven, self-motivated and make us all proud.

—Les Brown
Author of *Live Your Dreams*

PREFACE

Victory is defined by Webster's dictionary as, "Success in defeating an enemy or opponent or in overcoming difficulties." Young people are faced with many challenges and obstacles today: alcohol, deception, drugs, gang violence, peer pressure, gender identity, sex, suicide, unwed pregnancy, and a host of other stumbling blocks. These hurdles seem designed to keep today's youth from succeeding. *VICTORY 4 Youth! 7 Keys to Succeeding Against the Odds* provides young people with the essentials they need to overcome obstacles, reach goals, and fulfill dreams.

The seven complete sessions deal with:

Vision

Integrity

Courage

Thinking

Opportunity

Responsibility

Yes, You Can!

If young people are going to realize their full potential, they must create a larger *vision* of themselves beyond their present circumstances and mental conditioning. They must operate their lives from a foundation of *integrity*. They must have the *courage* to stand up for what they believe in and what they know is right. They must use the power of their minds and start *thinking* for themselves. They must become enterprising and create their own *opportunities*. They must stop making excuses and accept full *responsibility* for their lives. And they must believe in themselves and listen to their heart which says *"Yes, You Can!"* live your dreams.

VICTORY 4 Youth! 7 Keys to Succeeding Against the Odds is a self-help book for young people and people who are young at heart. This is not a book just to be read; it's a workbook that encourages the reader to get involved and to become an active force in creating his or her desired future. This program is highly flexible. Each session covers one fundamental principle, gives a real-life example of an individual who practices that principle, and includes exercises to reinforce it. Each session builds on the previous one and at the same time each session can also stand alone.

VICTORY 4 Youth! 7 Keys to Succeeding Against the Odds can be used effectively in a variety of ways: Individual study, informal discussion groups, retreats, and workshops. Several other learning possibilities exist depending on the creativity and objectives of the user.

INTRODUCTION

WARNING! DO NOT READ THIS BOOK—unless you are serious about becoming all that you can be. This book is only for those few individuals who truly have a burning desire to realize their full potential. Only *one* out of every ten individuals who reads this book will **do** what it takes to succeed. Are you the one? It doesn't matter what color you are. It doesn't matter what gender you are. It doesn't matter where you were born. It doesn't matter where you grew up. It doesn't matter what has happened to you in the past. And it doesn't matter if people do not believe in you. All that matters is that you believe in yourself and that you are committed to paying the price to succeed.

If you're ready to maximize your potential, this book could change your life forever…for the better. Booker T. Washington said, "Success always leaves footprints." This book contains the "footprints" that others have followed to make themselves successful.

Please understand. Success takes work—and that work must come from you! The only place that success comes *before* work is in the dictionary! You must *earn* the success you expect. That's where this book, **VICTORY 4 Youth! 7 Keys to Succeeding Against the Odds**, comes into play. This book will help you create the future you expect for yourself. This is both a book to read, and a book to "do." The exercises in this book are easier to read than they are to do, because to "do" requires self-discipline and commitment to your goal(s).

Do you want to succeed or do you expect to succeed? There is a big difference between *"wanting"* something and *"expecting"* something. "I *want*" shows up in conversation; "I *expect*" shows up in behavior. When people say, "I *want* _____," what they're really saying is "It would be nice to have _____ as long as I don't have to work for it." On the other hand, when people say, "I *expect* _____," what they're really saying is, "I am willing to "do" what it takes to get _____." There are a lot of young people who say, "I *want* to be successful"; however, very few say, "I *expect* to be successful." What do you say?

Here's what I know about you, without even knowing you personally: **"You were born to succeed!"** Everything you need to succeed is inside you. The following story illustrates my point. There is an old legend that suggests at one time all men on earth were gods, but the men so sinned and abused the Divine that Brahma, the god of all gods, decided that the godhead should be taken away from man and hidden somewhere where he would never find it again to abuse it. One god said, "Let's bury it deep in the earth." Brahma said, "No, man will dig down in the earth and find it." Another god said, "Then let's put it in the deepest ocean." Brahma said, "No, man will learn to dive and find it someday." A third god suggested, "Why don't we hide it on the highest mountain." Brahma said, "No, man can climb the highest mountain. I have a better place. Let's hide it down in man himself. He will never think to look there."

You have been blessed with everything you need to succeed. However, it's up to *you* to make it happen. No one owes you anything; you owe yourself. Let me say that again, "you owe yourself." If you *expect* to make your way to prosperity and a successful life, you need to: Have a vision, operate with integrity, express your courage, think for yourself, create your opportunities, accept full responsibility, and believe that yes, you can. If you're ready for greatness, let's get started!

VISION

"Where there is no vision, the people perish."

—Proverbs, 29:18

The "V" in VICTORY stands for:
VISION

Where do you see yourself in the next five, ten, fifteen years? If you don't have a vision for your life, then you are destined to live an average life. Vision is more than seeing with your eyes; it is seeing with your imagination. Albert Einstein said, **"Imagination is the preview of what is to come in your life."** Vision is the ability to create a clear mental picture of what the future will look like. Your vision describes the perfect future for you to attain. It provides purpose and direction while forcing you to break through self-imposed limitations. Creating and holding a clear mental picture in your mind of your desired future will activate your creative juices and produce the desire and energy to take action. Your imagination is the most powerful force in human existence. So, go ahead; dream a little.

Benjamin Carson grew up in the inner-city of Detroit. His future didn't look bright. He didn't have much motivation and his grades were terrible. At age eight, he was labeled the class dummy. However, Ben had a vision for his life: He wanted to be a doctor. Ben's mother never gave up on him. "You weren't born to be a failure, Bennie. You can do it!" And she pushed him, turning off the TV and making him read at least two books a week. Ben's grades improved. But then, in a fit of anger, he lost his temper and almost stabbed one of his best friends. Would he ever become the doctor he had envisioned as a young boy? Yes, and not only did he become a doctor, Ben Carson gained worldwide recognition for his part in the first successful separation of Siamese twins joined at the back of the head. The operation was extremely complex and delicate. It took five months of planning and preparation, and 22 hours in the operating room. Ben Carson, M.D. went on to become a director of pediatrics neurosurgery at Johns Hopkins Hospital, and the 17th United States Secretary of Housing and Urban Development. He also has become known for encouraging young people to set and meet goals by visiting schools and sharing his love for learning. He is the author of *Gifted Hands* and *Think Big* and the subject of a documentary film.

Vision is defined by Webster's dictionary as "The faculty of sight, unusual ability in foreseeing what is going to happen, a mental image created by the imagination."

Let your imagination go wild and complete the following sentences:

If I could be anything I wanted to be, I'd be _____

_____

If I had ten million dollars, I would _____

_____

I have always wanted to visit _____

_____

I always wanted to know how to _____

_____

My life will be great when _____

_____

One thing I'd really like to experience in my life would be _____

_____

I would like to be the kind of person that everybody describes as _____

_____

STIMULATING THE SENSES

Now that you have activated your imagination, take a few moments and imagine yourself living your dream. It would be helpful if you close your eyes, take a few deep breaths and relax. Now place yourself in the future as if you are looking out of your own eyes at this new, victorious life. What are you **doing**? What do you **see**? What do you **hear**? What do you **smell**? What do you **taste**? What are you **touching?** And how does all of this make you **feel**?

Describe (in detail) what you:

Are doing (for example: running your own business, performing on stage, helping people in a foreign country, etc.) _____

_____

_____

_____

_____

_____

See (for example: your beautiful home, your name up in lights, snow-capped mountains, etc.) _____

_____

_____

_____

_____

Hear (for example: the sound of your own private jet, the roar of the crowd, the sound of the ocean, etc.) _____

_____

_____

_____

_____

Smell (for example: your favorite fragrance, freshly cut flowers, hot apple pie, etc.)

_____

_____

_____

_____

Taste (for example: freshly squeezed orange juice, caviar, home-made ice cream, etc.)

_____

_____

_____

_____

Touch (for example: fine fabric, beautiful sculptures, animals, etc.) _____

_____

_____

_____

_____

_____

CREATING YOUR VISION

You must create a larger vision of yourself beyond your present circumstances and mental conditioning. Your vision must be strong enough to keep drawing you toward it, no matter what happens. Remember: "All things are possible to those who believe."

Write down your vision of the future.

_____

_____

_____

_____

_____

Describe (in detail) how your vision of the future makes you feel.

_____

_____

_____

_____

_____

_____

_____

_____

> "One essential ingredient for being an original in the day of copies is courageous vision."
>
> **—Charles Swindoll**

Write down five things that you have to *start* doing in order to make your vision a reality.

1. _____

2. _____

3. _____

4. _____

5. _____

Write down five things that you have to *stop* doing in order to make your vision a reality.

1. _____

2. _____

3. _____

4. _____

5. _____

Write down five things that you have to *continue* doing in order to make your vision a reality.

1. _____

2. _____

3. _____

4. _____

5. _____

SUCCESSFUL PEOPLE SET GOALS

Once you understand how important it is to have a vision for your life, you must set some *goals* in order to make your vision a reality.

The purpose of goals is to focus your attention, give your life direction, and create activity. Your mind will not reach toward achievement until it has clear objectives.

A study of Yale University graduates some years ago discovered that only three percent had *written* goals in life. Twenty years later, a follow-up study revealed that the three percent who had written down their goals had healthier relationships, better jobs, and accumulated more wealth, than the other 97 percent combined!

If you want to enjoy a successful and well-balanced life, you should set goals in each of the nine major areas of your life.

Career: Goals for the type of work that you would love to do.

Education: Goals for the level and type of education you want, or need.

Family: Goals for healthy family relationships.

Financial: Goals for the amount of money you want to earn.

Material: Goals for the things you want—car, house, etc.

Physical: Goals for your overall health and physical fitness.

Recreational: Goals for rest and relaxation—hobbies, travel, etc.

Social: Goals for your contribution to society.

Spiritual: Goals for peace of mind and spiritual fulfillment.

SETTING AND ACHIEVING GOALS

When you write down your goals, make sure they're **"S.M.A.R.T."**

Specific,

Measurable,

Achievable,

Relevant, and

Time-Bound

DEFINING THE TERMS

- *Specific* goals are detailed and focused. A goal is specific when you know exactly what you're going to accomplish and achieve. Being specific means spelling out the details.

- *Measurable* goals are quantifiable. A measurable goal provides a standard for comparison, the means to an end, a specific result; it is limiting. Each goal must be measurable—it must have a method for comparison that indicates when the goal is reached.

- *Achievable* goals should be challenging but also possible to attain. If your goal is too easy, you won't stretch yourself to grow. If your goal is too difficult, you may get discouraged and set yourself up for failure.

- *Relevant* goals should be related to what you're trying to accomplish long term. If your goal does not align with your overall direction, you won't gain momentum toward your larger plan or vision.

- *Time-bound* goals have a deadline for when they should be accomplished. People generally put off doing things if no deadline is set because human nature always finds something else to do that has a higher priority.

HERE ARE SOME EXAMPLES OF "S.M.A.R.T." GOALS:

- "I will show up on time to every class every day this month."
- "I will contribute to a discussion in every class at least one time per week."
- "I will turn in all assignments on time for the entire semester."
- "I will study for three hours per week for the entire semester."
- "I will limit gaming and screen time to two hours a day max."
- "I will volunteer for five hours this semester."
- "I will get a part-time job by the end of June."

6 STEPS
TO GOAL SETTING AND
ACCOMPLISHMENT

1. Write down your goal, making sure it's **"S.M.A.R.T."**.

2. List the benefits you will enjoy after reaching your goal.

3. List the obstacles you will have to overcome to reach your goal.

4. List the education, knowledge, and skills required to accomplish your goal.

5. Identify the people and organizations that can help you attain your goal.

6. Write down your plan of action for achieving your goal.

"Goal "setting" is important...
Goal "doing" is more important."

—Anonymous

GOAL WORKSHEET

Write down your **"S.M.A.R.T."** goal: _____

_____

_____

_____

_____

_____

_____

_____

List three benefits you will enjoy as a result of reaching your goal.

1. _____

2. _____

3. _____

List three obstacles you will have to overcome to reach your goal.

1. _____

2. _____

3. _____

List the education, knowledge, and skills you will have to acquire to accomplish your goal.

Education: _____

Knowledge: _____

Skills: _____

Identify the people and organizations whose assistance you will need to accomplish your goal.

- ● _____

- ● _____

- ● _____

- ● _____

- ● _____

- ● _____

Write down your plan of action for achieving your goal.

_____

_____

_____

_____

_____

_____

VISION ACTION STEPS

Write down one goal that you *will* reach within the **next six months**. _____

_____

_____

_____

Write down one thing you *will* do:

- **Today** that will get you a little closer to your goal.

_____

_____

_____

- **Next week** that will get you even closer to your goal.

_____

_____

_____

- **Next month** that will get you even closer to your goal.

_____

_____

_____

VISION SESSION SUMMARY

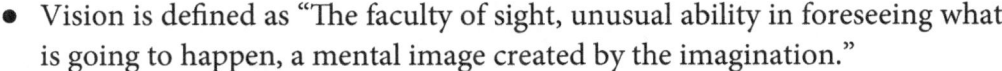

- Vision is defined as "The faculty of sight, unusual ability in foreseeing what is going to happen, a mental image created by the imagination."
- Vision is the ability to create a clear mental picture of what the future will look like.
- You must create a larger vision of yourself beyond your present circumstances and mental conditioning.
- Goals focus your attention, give your life direction, and create activity.
- For a successful and well-balanced life, set goals in each of the nine major areas of your life.
- Set **S.M.A.R.T**. goals: **S**pecific, **M**easurable, **A**chievable, **R**elevant, and **T**ime-Bound.

REFLECTIONS

Use this page to write down any thoughts and takeaways that come to mind as you *"reflect"* on the session you've just completed.

_____

_____

_____

_____

_____

_____

_____

_____

_____

_____

_____

_____

_____

_____

_____

SESSION TWO

INTEGRITY

"Integrity is doing the right thing, even when no one is watching."

—C.S. Lewis

Based on your *current* value system, answer the following questions.

- Would you lie to cover up something you did wrong?

  Yes ❑ No ❑ It depends ❑

- Would you avoid telling your best friend the truth for the sake of peace?

  Yes ❑ No ❑ It depends ❑

- Would you cheat to pass a test that you did not study for?

  Yes ❑ No ❑ It depends ❑

- Would you stand up for something you believe in, even if it meant that you would be unpopular?

  Yes ❑ No ❑ It depends ❑

- If you found a wallet that contained ten 100-dollar bills, credit cards, and a driver's license, would you return it with everything you found in it?

  Yes ❑ No ❑ It depends ❑

The "I" in VICTORY stands for:
INTEGRITY

What values (personal traits or characteristics) do you look for and admire in a *true* friend? If you're like most young people, integrity is at the top of your list. Integrity is the deepest form of honesty. In the business world, studies show integrity ranks as the number one quality sought in every field. Persons with integrity are the same at home and at school, with family and friends. They stand firmly for their convictions in the face of tremendous personal pressure, always give others the credit and respect that is rightfully theirs, and are honest and open about who they really are. People with integrity have a core set of values that guide the choices they make **regardless** of the situation or environment in which they find themselves at the moment. They do not base their decisions on whether or not they are politically correct. Instead, they do what they do because it is the right thing to do.

Seven-year-old Tanner Munsey's reputation for honesty earned him a mention in *Sports Illustrated* magazine's "Scoreboard" column. During a T-ball game in Wellington, Florida, first baseman Tanner Munsey fielded a ground ball and tried to tag the runner going from first base to second. The umpire called the runner out, but Tanner immediately ran up to her and said, "Ma'am, I didn't tag the runner." The umpire awarded the runner second base. For his honesty, Tanner was given the game ball by his coach.

In a game two weeks later, a similar play occurred. It was the same umpire, and Tanner was playing shortstop. This time, the umpire thought Tanner missed tagging the runner going to third base and called the runner safe. Tanner glanced at the umpire, tossed the ball to the catcher without saying a word, and trotted back to his position. The umpire sensed something wasn't right.

"Did you tag the runner?" she asked Tanner.

"Yes," he answered.

The umpire immediately reversed her decision and called the runner out. The umpire's decision drew jeers from the crowd and protests from the opposing coaches. To settle things down, the umpire explained what had happened two weeks earlier and said, "If the kid is that honest, I have to give it to him."

> *Integrity* is defined by Webster's dictionary as "Strict adherence to a standard of value or conduct, personal honesty and independence, completeness, soundness."

In order to live a life of integrity, you must create a set of personal values. These values will then become the guiding principles for how you will operate your life.

Your *values* answer the question, **"What's important to me?"** Your values are the standards that influence every aspect of your life—especially your relationships with family and friends, your attitude and behavior toward money, and your commitments to others.

Partial List of Values

Achievement/ Success	Autonomy	Beauty	Challenge	Communication
Competence	Competition	Courage	Creativity	Curiosity
Decisiveness	Dependability	Discipline	Diversity	Effectiveness
Empathy	Equality	Family	Flexibility	Freedom
Friendship	Growth	Happiness	Harmony	Health
Honesty/Integrity	Hope	Humor	Independence	Innovation
Intelligence	Love/Affection	Loyalty	Open-mindedness	Patience
Perseverance	Power	Productivity	Prosperity/Wealth	Quality
Recognition	Respect	Risk-Taking	Security	Service
Simplicity	Spirituality/ Faith	Strength	Teamwork	Trust
Truth	Variety	Wisdom		

Note: Use the two blank boxes above to fill in values you may have that are not listed.

VALUES WORKSHEET

Write one value *(from the partial list of values on page 42)* in each square that indicates how important that value is in your life.

ALWAYS VALUED	OFTEN VALUED	SOMETIMES VALUED	SELDOM VALUED	LEAST VALUED

Write down your top five values from the *"always value"* column on the *"values worksheet"* on page 43.

1. _____

2. _____

3. _____

4. _____

5. _____

Remember: A higher-order value will always take priority over a lower-order value. If you are ever forced to choose between acting on one value or another, choose the value that is the highest on your list.

After writing down each value, write down a specific example of how you have (or will) demonstrate that value in your life.

1. _____

_____

2. _____

_____

3. _____

_____

4. _____

_____

5. _____

_____

Write down the names of three people *(living or dead)* whom you admire for their qualities of integrity, honesty, courage, trustworthiness, or wisdom.

- _____

- _____

- _____

Think of a difficult situation that you are dealing with right now, and then ask yourself:

"What would _____ **do in my situation?"**

(insert one of the names above)

THE INTEGRITY CHALLENGE

> There are no degrees of integrity;
> you are either honest or dishonest.

What is integrity?

_____

_____

_____

_____

Why is integrity important?

_____

_____

_____

_____

What is an example of integrity?

_____

_____

_____

_____

Remember: *The right way is often the road least traveled. The street named "Integrity" is not a crowded street. To distinguish yourself before the world only requires that you set yourself apart from the crowd. As one of Spike Lee's films suggests,* **"Do The Right Thing."**

INTEGRITY ACTION STEPS

Write down one area of your life where you lack integrity.

_____

_____

_____

What is this lack of integrity costing you?

_____

_____

_____

_____

_____

Now, write down what you *will* do to become a person of integrity in that area of your life.

_____

_____

_____

_____

_____

INTEGRITY SESSION SUMMARY

- Integrity is defined as "Strict adherence to a standard of value or conduct, personal honesty and independence, completeness, soundness."

- Integrity is the number one quality sought in every area of life.

- In order to live a life of integrity, you must create a set of personal values.

- Values answer the question, "What's important to me?"

- Values influence your relationships with your family and friends, your attitude and behavior toward money, and your commitments to others.

- A higher-order value will always take precedence over a lower-order value.

- Remember to ask yourself the question:

  "What would _____ do in my situation?"

- There are no degrees of integrity; you are either honest or dishonest.

REFLECTIONS

Use this page to write down any thoughts and takeaways that come to mind as you *"reflect"* on the session you've just completed.

_____

_____

_____

_____

_____

_____

_____

_____

_____

_____

_____

_____

_____

_____

_____

_____

COURAGE

"Courage may be the most important of all virtues, because without it one cannot practice any other virtue with consistency."

—Maya Angelou

The "C" in VICTORY stands for:
COURAGE

Do you *expect* to experience all that life has for you? If you *expect* to live a victorious life, you must master fear and develop courage. How? As best-selling author Susan Jeffers says, **"Feel The Fear And Do It Anyway."** It doesn't take any effort to be like everyone else. However, it takes courage to be great, to be different from the crowd—to be yourself. It takes courage to say "No" to alcohol, cigarettes, and drugs. It takes courage to say "No" to gang violence, peer pressure, and premarital sex. It takes courage to sacrifice; to study for hours when you could be relaxing with your friends; to practice when you're sick or tired. It takes courage to stand by your convictions when all those around you have no convictions. It takes courage to pursue your dreams. Deep inside you lies all the courage you will ever need to fulfill your purpose.

Dave Dravecky is a synonym for courage. Dave grew up playing baseball in his backyard in Youngstown, Ohio. Since the age of seven, he dreamed of making it to the big leagues. And after years of hard work, his dream became a reality. Dave wasn't just a major-league pitcher; he was one of the best. In 1983 he was selected to pitch in the All-Star game, and pitched two scoreless innings. In 1984 he pitched in the World Series, and pitched ten and two-thirds scoreless innings. And in 1987 he pitched a shutout in the National League Championship. In the fall of 1987, while pitching for the San Francisco Giants, Dave noticed a lump in his left arm. Was it cancer? Yes! Surgery removed one half of the deltoid muscle in Dave's arm, and the doctors said he would never pitch again. However, with extraordinary faith and courage, Dave proved them wrong. After a rehabilitation period, Dave was back pitching in the major leagues! The New York Times said Dave's comeback was, "One of the most dramatic moments in sports history." Dave Dravecky, a former all-star pitcher for the San Francisco Giants, went on to speak across the country, sharing his story of hope with thousands. He is the author of the best-selling book *Comeback.* He is also the subject of the documentary film "Dravecky: A Story of Courage and Grace."

Courage is defined by Webster's dictionary as "Ability to conquer fear or despair."

Most of us experience three types of fear: 1. The fear of failure, which causes us to think and say, **"I can't."** For example: "I can't get an "A" in math." 2. The fear of rejection, which causes us to think and say, **"I have to."** For example: "I have to get straight "A's" or I'm a failure." 3. The fear of success, which causes us to think and say, **"What will success cost me?"** For example: If I get straight "A's" will I be bullied for being smart?

In order to overcome our fears, we must face them and take action. Understand that it's okay to be afraid. Most intelligent people are afraid of something. Mark Twain said, "Courage is resistance to fear, mastery of fear—not absence of fear."

THREE TYPES OF COURAGE:

1. The courage to start, to step out in faith. This is the courage to move out of your comfort zone and try something new and different.

2. The courage to continue, to endure. This is the courage to persist until you make it. When the going gets tough, the tough *keep* going.

3. The courage to maintain your convictions. This is the courage to stand for what you believe in, and to stand for what is right, even if you have to stand alone.

"I learned that courage was not the absence of fear, but the triumph over it."

—Nelson Mandela

INCREASING YOUR SELF-ESTEEM

One of the keys to courage is confidence. And confidence is a result of healthy self-esteem. Self-esteem is the value you place on yourself. It is the way you think and feel about yourself and it's measured by the way you act. To enhance your self-esteem, you have to work primarily on changing "inside." Here are ten ways to increase your self-esteem.

1. **Accept Praise and Recognition.** When you are praised or recognized for any reason, accept the compliment by saying, "*Thank you.*"

2. **Don't Compare Yourself To Others.** You are a '*unique*' individual. There is no one else like you. Set your own standards. Compare what you have accomplished with what you are capable of accomplishing.

3. **Don't Take Failure Personally**. Don't <u>interpret</u> '*you have failed*' (a comment about behavior) as '*you are a failure*' (a comment about identity). You are **more** than the results you produce.

4. **Don't Try To Be Perfect.** Perfection doesn't exist. Accept yourself as an imperfect, worthwhile person; however, keep striving to become the best version of yourself . Also, realize that some people may not like you as much as you would like.

5. **Focus On Your Strengths.** Everyone has been blessed with a unique combination of abilities, gifts, and talents. This means there are some things you do well, and there are some things you will not do so well. Continue to build on your strengths.

6. **Keep A "Success" Journal.** Small successes build confidence. Write down and review the times when you have felt confident and worthy. Use your imagination to create pictures in your mind of those positive times. Reviewing your journal and visualizing positive experiences will help in those times when you're feeling a little down.

7. **Keep Up Your Appearance.** Always dress and look your best. The better you look, the better you'll feel.

8. **Practice Positive Self-Talk.** When you talk to yourself and to others about yourself, <u>always</u> use affirmative and positive adjectives and adverbs—i.e., "*I am a confident and positive individual.*"

9. **Practice The "As If" Technique**. Act *'as if'* you already have high self-esteem in a situation where you want this to be true. Also, model the behavior of those individuals who have high self-esteem.

10. **See Yourself Liking Yourself**. Look in the mirror, smile at your reflection and say, "_____, I like you!"

        (Insert your name)

"Have the courage to be different without being contrary—without flaunting your independence. The quality that makes us interesting, that makes us outstanding personalities, is the courage to be ourselves."

—Anonymous

PREPARATION IS THE KEY

Research indicates that one key factor in acquiring the ability to act courageously is thoughtful advance **preparation**. Studies show that courageous behavior is the result of two kinds of preparation:

1. **Technical preparedness.** Your self-confidence and self-esteem can be increased by knowing that you have thoroughly prepared yourself for the assignment at hand. (For example, if you're going to take a test next week, then focus on becoming thoroughly familiar with the subject matter.)

2. **Emotional preparedness.** You must also prepare yourself by anticipating how you will feel when you have to carry out your assignment. (For example, you must anticipate the experience of taking a test which will have an impact on your overall grade for the class.)

Write down what you are afraid of:

- _____
- _____
- _____
- _____
- _____
- _____

Now, relative to the above fears, answer the following three questions:

1. **How does this fear keep me from moving forward in life?** (For example: If you have a fear of doing well in science class, because you don't understand the basics, you'll be less likely to study and do the assignments. Thus, you may miss out on a great opportunity in the science field.)

   _____

   _____

   _____

   _____

   _____

2. **How does this fear help me?** (For example: In order to do well in your science class, you're going to have to study, work hard, and ask for help.)

   _____

   _____

   _____

   _____

   _____

3. How would I benefit from conquering this fear? (For example: After doing well in your science class, you'll realize that if you apply yourself, you have the ability to learn whatever you want to learn.)

_____

_____

_____

_____

_____

_____

Write down why you think it is important to be courageous:

_____

_____

_____

_____

_____

_____

Write down one time when you were courageous:

_____

_____

_____

_____

_____

_____

_____

Write down how it felt to be courageous:

_____

_____

_____

_____

_____

_____

Using your imagination, complete the following exercise.

If I had the courage I would:

1. _____

2. _____

3. _____

4. _____

5. _____

Now that you have completed the above exercise, it's time to master your fear and develop courage. You must understand that courage follows action. Eleanor Roosevelt said, "You gain strength, courage, and confidence by every experience in which you really stop to look fear in the face…. The danger lies in refusing to face the fear, in not daring to come to grips with it…. You must make yourself succeed every time. You must do the thing you think you cannot do." Fear is conquered by action. Visualize yourself taking action, conquering your fears, and pursuing your dreams. Now is the time to take charge of your life and make it happen. How? As the slogan of a famous shoe company suggests, "**Just Do It!**"

> *"Courage is the capacity to confront what*
> *can be imagined."*
>
> **—Leo Rosten**

COMPLETE THE FOLLOWING SENTENCES:

It takes courage to act _____ .

It takes courage to ask _____ .

It takes courage to be _____ .

It takes courage to believe _____ .

It takes courage to care _____ .

It takes courage to continue _____ .

It takes courage to do _____ .

It takes courage to distinguish _____ .

It takes courage to end _____ .

It takes courage to endure _____ .

It takes courage to face _____ .

It takes courage to follow _____ .

It takes courage to go _____ .

It takes courage to grow _____ .

It takes courage to have _____ .

It takes courage to hear _____ .

It takes courage to identify _____ .

It takes courage to include _____ .

It takes courage to listen _____ .

It takes courage to love _____ .

It takes courage to march _____ .

It takes courage to make _____ .

It takes courage to obey _____ .

It takes courage to persist _____ .

It takes courage to practice _____ .

It takes courage to quit _____ .

It takes courage to reprove _____ .

It takes courage to risk _____ .

It takes courage to say _____ .

It takes courage to share _____ .

It takes courage to stand _____ .

It takes courage to start _____ .

It takes courage to tell _____ .

It takes courage to think _____ .

It takes courage to try _____ .

It takes courage to visit _____ .

It takes courage to wait _____ .

It takes courage to walk _____ .

> *"Courage is the price that life exacts for granting peace.*
> *The soul that knows it not, knows no release*
> *from little things; knows not the livid loneliness of fear,*
> *nor mountain heights where bitter joy can hear*
> *the sound of wings."*
>
> **—Amelia Earhart**

COURAGE ACTION STEPS

Write down one of your biggest fears.

_____

_____

_____

Now, write out a detailed plan of action describing how you *will* (within the **next 30 days**) *prepare* yourself both *technically* and *emotionally* to face and conquer one of your biggest fears.

_____

_____

_____

_____

_____

_____

_____

_____

_____

_____

_____

COURAGE SESSION SUMMARY

- Courage is defined as "Ability to conquer fear or despair."

- It takes courage to be great, different from the crowd—to be yourself.

- It's OK to be afraid. Most intelligent people are afraid of something.

- Courage is expressed in three ways: 1. The courage to start, 2. The courage to continue, and 3. The courage to maintain your convictions.

- Courageous behavior is the result of two kinds of preparation: 1. Technical preparation, and 2. Emotional preparation.

- Fear is conquered by action.

- FEAR is an acrostic that stands for: **F**alse **E**xpectations **A**ppearing **R**eal.

REFLECTIONS

Use this page to write down any thoughts and takeaways that come to mind as you *"reflect"* on the session you've just completed.

_____

_____

_____

_____

_____

_____

_____

_____

_____

_____

_____

_____

_____

_____

_____

_____

_____

SESSION FOUR

THINKING

"For as he thinketh in his heart, so is he."

—Proverbs, 23:7

The "T" in VICTORY stands for:
THINKING

Are you in control of your thought life? Your thoughts are the only thing over which you can exercise complete control. Whatever you think about today and tomorrow, next month and next year, will shape your life and determine your future. Earl Nightingale said that the strangest secret is, **"We become what we think about."** Your mind will absorb any idea that it is repeatedly subjected to, positive or negative, right or wrong, good or bad. Once absorbed, your subconscious mind goes to work to create the circumstances that will make your dominating thoughts a reality. You cannot directly choose your circumstances; however, you can choose your thoughts, and so indirectly shape your circumstances. Whether you like it or not, you are the sum total of your own thoughts. You are not what you think you are; *but what you think, you are.*

Becky Tirabassi almost ruined her life by <u>not</u> thinking about the consequences. Becky was born in Berea, Ohio. Wanting to be popular and escape some of her family problems, Becky took her first drink on the Fourth of July when she was fifteen years old. As a teenager, Becky just wanted to fit in and be accepted. But she never felt pretty enough, she wasn't rich, and she didn't get along with her parents. To escape her problems, she began drinking—and felt confident and outgoing for the first time in her life. The search for fun and friends made her a teenage alcoholic. After graduating from high school, Becky started college at Bowling Green State University. She dropped out of college the following year. By the time Becky was twenty-one, drugs and alcohol had taken over her life. Finally, on the verge of suicide, she admitted she was an alcoholic and asked for help. Becky Tirabassi went from being an alcoholic to an author and fitness instructor, from a lost and confused teen-ager to a mature woman. She has written seven books, produced an award-winning workout video, and founded *My Partner Ministries*. She has traveled throughout the United States and Canada as a full-time speaker touching the lives of thousands of people with her powerful message.

Thinking is defined by Webster's dictionary as "To formulate (a thought) in the mind, to reflect on: ponder, to exercise the power of reason, to have view (about): believe, to recall: remember."

Since you are the product of your dominating thoughts, it is necessary that you evaluate everything and everyone in your life who influences your thinking. You cannot accept an opinion offered to you unless it is based on facts or sound hypoth-eses about the facts. Independent thinkers never act on the advice and opinions of others without giving those viewpoints the closest scrutiny; they permit no one to do their thinking for them. They obtain facts, information, and counsel from oth-ers; however, they retain the right to accept or reject it in whole or in part.

Think about your self-talk. Self-talk can be defined as the constant conversation that you have with yourself as you judge and interpret your own experience. To become a successful person, it is imperative that you monitor and control your self-talk every minute of the day. Your thoughts and feelings will determine your actions. Since your conscious mind can hold only *one* thought at a time, either realistic or negative, keep your thoughts and words realistic and consistent with your goals. Keep your mind focused on what you want to be, do, and have. **Never say**, "I'm too (afraid, dumb, stupid, ugly, etc.) to …"

Replace your *"negative"* thinking with *"realistic"* thinking.

Negative Thinking	Realistic Thinking
"I can't"	"I Can"
"I'll try"	"I will"
"I quit"	"I'll persevere"
"I have to"	"I want to"
"I have a problem"	"I have an opportunity"

Think about your friends. Evaluate the type of relationship that you have with each one of your friends. Are the people you associate with positive or negative? Are you becoming a better person because you associate with them? Do they encourage you or tell you what you "can't" do?

List your five closest friends and make a decision to either *"continue"* or *"end"* the relationship. **This is your life we are talking about;** you can't afford to let anyone slow you down.

1. _____ Continue ❏ End ❏

2. _____ Continue ❏ End ❏

3. _____ Continue ❏ End ❏

4. _____ Continue ❏ End ❏

5. _____ Continue ❏ End ❏

Ending a relationship is never easy. It's been said that "Breaking up is hard to do." However, if you are not becoming a better person because of the relationship, then it's necessary that you bring it to an end. Surround yourself with positive people. You want to have relationships with individuals who will challenge you to grow emotionally, intellectually, and spiritually.

> *"Trust yourself. Think for yourself. Act for yourself. Speak for yourself. Be yourself. Imitation is suicide."*
>
> **—Marva Collins**

CHOOSING THE "RIGHT" FRIENDS

It is imperative that you choose your friends wisely. The people you choose to *"hang-out"* with will have a profound influence on who you become and what you will or will not do. There is an old saying: "Birds of a feather flock together." Make sure you're soaring with eagles and not strutting with turkeys!

Now that you understand the importance of choosing your friends with great care, describe in detail the type of friend you would like to have.

I would like the type of friend who _____

_____

_____

_____

_____

_____

_____

_____

Now, write down five places where you can find the type of friend you just described who will reinforce your positive qualities.

1. _____

2. _____

3. _____

4. _____

5. _____

A little girl asked her father to pick a flower for her. That was simple enough. But when she said, "Now put it back," the father experienced a baffling helplessness he never knew before. "How can you explain that it cannot be done?" He thought. "How can you make clear to young people that there are some things which once broken, once mutilated, can never be replaced or mended?"

Think before you act! Life is about choices. And the choices you make today will dictate the life you live tomorrow. You want to make intelligent choices that will have a positive impact on your future. Every choice you make should get you closer to your goal. A key to making intelligent choices is to *think* about the consequences in advance.

Write down six consequences of alcohol and drugs:

1. _____   2. _____

3. _____   4. _____

5. _____   6. _____

Write down six consequences of sex:

1. _____   2. _____

3. _____   4. _____

5. _____   6. _____

Write down six consequences of gang violence:

1. _____   2. _____

3. _____   4. _____

5. _____   6. _____

Write down six consequences of following the crowd:

1. _____   2. _____

3. _____   4. _____

5. _____   6. _____

Write down six consequences of dropping out of school:

1. _____   2. _____

3. _____   4. _____

5. _____   6. _____

Write down six consequences of wasting your free time:

1. _____   2. _____

3. _____   4. _____

5. _____   6. _____

Write down the importance of thinking for yourself:

_____

_____

_____

_____

_____

_____

In addition to thinking about your self-talk, thinking about your friends, and thinking before you act, it's important to think about the good things in your life to maintain an optimistic perspective.

Think about what you are grateful for. You should never let a day pass without taking a few minutes to give thanks for your blessings. Gratitude is a matter of comparison. Compare circumstances and events against what they might have been; you will become aware that no matter how bad things are, they could be much worse—and you will be grateful that they aren't.

Three phrases should be among the most common in your daily usage. They are: **"Thank you," "I'm grateful," and "I appreciate."** True gratitude requires you to express appreciation in more than words. Sincere gratitude will be backed up with action. If you feel grateful, how can you express your gratitude?

Write down five things you can do to express your gratitude.

1. _____

2. _____

3. _____

4. _____

5. _____

"Finally, brethren, whatsoever things are true, whatsoever things are honest, whatsoever things are just, whatsoever things are pure, whatsoever things are lovely, whatsoever things are of good report; if there be any virtue, and if there be any praise, think on these things."

—Philippians, 4:8

GRATITUDE WORKSHEET

Write down the **people, places, things, and "other"** things you are grateful for. Some examples of *"other"* things: Challenges, freedom, health, etc.

People	Places	Things	Other

Now that you have your gratitude list, every time you have a negative thought, counter it with a thought of gratitude.

THINKING ACTION STEPS

Write down the names of two people who you appreciate.

- _____

- _____

Now, write down something that you *will* do **this week** to express your appreciation to each person. (**Hint**: Be creative.)

Person number one:

_____

_____

_____

_____

_____

Person number two:

_____

_____

_____

_____

_____

THINKING SESSION SUMMARY

- Thinking is defined as "To formulate (a thought) in the mind, to reflect on: ponder, to exercise the power of reason, to have view (about): believe, to recall: remember."

- Your thoughts are the only thing over which you have complete control.

- Whatever you think about today and tomorrow will shape your life and determine your future.

- The strangest secret: "We become what we think about."

- You cannot directly choose your circumstances; however, you can choose your thoughts, and so indirectly shape your circumstances.

- Evaluate everything and everyone in your life who influences your thinking.

- Think about your self-talk. Think about your friends. Think before you act. Think about what you are grateful for.

REFLECTIONS

Use this page to write down any thoughts and takeaways that come to mind as you *"reflect"* on the session you've just completed.

_____

_____

_____

_____

_____

_____

_____

_____

_____

_____

_____

_____

_____

_____

_____

_____

OPPORTUNITY

"The golden opportunity you are seeking is in yourself. It is not in your environment; it is not in luck or chance, or the help of others; it is in yourself alone."

—Orison Swett Marden

The "O" in VICTORY stands for:
OPPORTUNITY

Do you realize that you have the power to create more opportunities than you will ever find? George Bernard Shaw said, "The people who get on in this world are the people who get up and look for the circumstances they want, and, if they can't find them, make them." The responsibility is yours, you must do all you can in preparation for what you expect to come. Opportunity is not a matter of luck or chance—it is an attitude, a way of seeing the world. If you are confident enough, creative enough, disciplined enough, and skilled enough, there are no limits to the opportunities you can create. You create opportunities by seeing the possibilities, being prepared, and having the courage to act upon them. When you have the attitude that says, "No matter what happens to me, I will benefit from it," you will know and understand the truth: *You create opportunity.*

Kamaria Warren understands what creating opportunity is all about. At age seven, she started her entrepreneurial journey by launching her small business, Brown Girls Stationary (BGS). She made over $10,000.00 in profit that year. The idea for Brown Girl Stationary came to Kamaria after she and her mother went shopping for birthday invitations for her upcoming party. After searching and searching, they found no products representing Brown and Black girls. Instead of complaining, Kamaria set out to rectify the situation. Kamaria Warren is a teenage CEO whose company offers backpacks, t-shirts, notebooks, bedding, blankets, shower curtains, umbrellas, and party supplies for girls of color. Business is trending up and to the right; Black Girl Stationary has five employees and five volunteers. Brown Girls Stationary sells its products online, wholesale, and at local events. On average, BGS sells around

10,000 notebooks, 2,500 notepads, and 1,500 backpacks annually. Warren says, "I'm motivated by seeing other girls wear my stuff and being proud of who they are." Kamaria's motto is:

"Dear Brown girl, you have the ability to change the world." This hardworking CEO is doing her part to help young want-to-be entrepreneurs get started. She recently launched the Mini CEO Academy, a membership website that provides business videos and tools to empower aspiring kid entrepreneurs.

"ACRES OF DIAMONDS"

Years ago, when the first diamonds were being discovered in Africa, diamond fever spread across the continent like wildfire. Many people struck it rich in their search for the sparkling beauties, and they became millionaires overnight.

At this time, Lamar, a young black farmer in central Africa, was scratching out a moderate living on the land that he owned. However, the promise of great diamond wealth soon possessed Lamar, and one day he could no longer restrain his insatiable desire for diamonds and the lust to become a wealthy man. He sold his farm, packed a few essentials, and left his family in search of the magnificent stones.

His search was long and painful. He wandered throughout the African continent, battling insects and wild beasts. Sleeping in the elements, fighting the damp and cold, Lamar searched day after day, week after week, but found no diamonds. He became sick, penniless, and utterly discouraged. He felt there was nothing more to live for, so he threw himself into a raging river and drowned.

Meanwhile, back on the farm that Lamar had sold, the farmer who bought the land was working the soil one day and found a strange-looking stone in the small creek that ran across the farm. The farmer brought it into his farmhouse and placed it on the fireplace mantle as a curio.

Later, a visitor came to the farmer's home and noticed the unusual stone. He grasped the stone quickly and shouted excitedly at the farmer, "Do you know this is a diamond? It's one of the largest diamonds I've ever seen." Further investigation revealed that the entire farm was covered with magnificent diamonds. In fact, this farm turned out to be one of the richest and most productive diamond mines in the world, and the farmer became one of the wealthiest men in Africa.

> **Opportunity** is defined by Webster's dictionary as "A favorable combination of circumstances, a chance for advancement."

DISCOVERING YOUR OWN ACRES OF DIAMONDS

The person who truly knows himself or herself has an advantage over the rest of us. That's because in knowing yourself, you recognize the abilities, gifts and talents you possess that will benefit society, and you also realize the areas in which you need some improvement.

What activities do you most enjoy doing? _____

_____

_____

_____

_____

What subjects really interest you? _____

_____

_____

_____

_____

Time flies when you are doing what? _____

_____

_____

_____

What ability or skill comes easy and natural to you that could be your "diamond" in the rough? _____

_____

_____

_____

_____

_____

How you see yourself is directly related to the opportunities that you will create. Your self-image is the vehicle that either holds you back or drives you to be and do your best. There is nothing wrong with a healthy ego. If you don't think well of yourself, who else will? Write down at least ten things you like about yourself:

1. _____

2. _____

3. _____

4. _____

5. _____

6. _____

7. _____

8. _____

9. _____

10. _____

Write down abilities and skills that you have in each of the areas listed below. You will discover all the many talents you already have. After you complete this exercise, look at your list and think of opportunities you can create for yourself based on what you know and can do.

Academic _____

Artistic _____

Athletic _____

Domestic _____

Dramatic _____

Financial _____

Games _____

Literary _____

Musical _____

Social _____

Technological _____

Other _____

If you want a better life, you must become a better person. Write down at least ten areas in which you need some improvement. After you complete this exercise, choose *one* area and implement a plan of action for improving that area of your life. Once you are satisfied with your improvement, select another area and repeat the process. Do this for the entire list.

1. _____

2. _____

3. _____

4. _____

5. _____

6. _____

7. _____

8. _____

9. _____

10. _____

"The largest room in the world is the room for improvement."

—Anonymous

YOUR OPPORTUNITY TO SERVE

Life is about receiving and *giving*. You cannot achieve greatness without being of service. All great men and women became great because they gave some ability or talent in the service of others. In the words of John Bunyan, "You have not lived today until you have done something for someone who can never repay you."

Write down three things you can do to serve your family.

1. _____

2. _____

3. _____

Write down three things you can do to serve your school.

1. _____

2. _____

3. _____

Write down three things you can do to serve your community.

1. _____

2. _____

3. _____

> *"Try to forget yourself in the service of others. For when we think too much of ourselves and our own interest, we easily become despondent. But when we work for others, our efforts return to bless us."*
>
> **—Sidney Powell**

YOUR OPPORTUNITY TO RESPECT AND VALUE PEOPLE WHO ARE *DIFFERENT* FROM YOU.

Opportunity comes in all different shapes, sizes, and colors. There are two reasons why it is important to respect and value people who are different from you: 1. It's simply the *"right"* thing to do. 2. Oftentimes the help you will need to make the most of an opportunity will come from someone who is different from you.

Write down ten things you can do to show that you respect and value individuals who are different (i.e. age, ethnicity, gender, physical abilities, race, etc.) from you.

1. _____

2. _____

3. _____

4. _____

5. _____

6. _____

7. _____

8. _____

9. _____

10. _____

OPPORTUNITY WORKSHEET

Make a list of opportunities that you have to earn extra income for yourself.

- _____
- _____
- _____
- _____
- _____
- _____
- _____
- _____
- _____
- _____
- _____
- _____
- _____

Make a list of opportunities that you have to gain experience in an area that you find interesting.

- _____
- _____
- _____
- _____
- _____
- _____
- _____
- _____
- _____
- _____
- _____
- _____
- _____
- _____
- _____
- _____
- _____
- _____
- _____
- _____

OPPORTUNITY ACTION STEPS

Write down one thing that you *will* do **this month** to serve:

Your family _____

_____

_____

_____

_____

_____

Your school _____

_____

_____

_____

_____

Your community _____

_____

_____

_____

_____

OPPORTUNITY SESSION SUMMARY

- Opportunity is defined as "A favorable combination of circumstances, a chance for advancement."

- You create opportunity.

- Your "acres of diamonds" are inside you.

- How you see yourself is directly related to the opportunities that you will create.

- If you want a better life, you must become a better person.

- Life is about receiving and giving. You cannot achieve greatness without being of service.

- Opportunity comes in all different shapes, sizes, and colors.

REFLECTIONS

Use this page to write down any thoughts and takeaways that come to mind as you *"reflect"* on the session you've just completed.

_____

_____

_____

_____

_____

_____

_____

_____

_____

_____

_____

_____

_____

_____

_____

_____

RESPONSIBILITY

"The price of greatness is responsibility."

—Winston Churchill

The "R" in VICTORY stands for:
RESPONSIBILITY

Have you matured to the point where you accept total responsibility for your life, or are you still making excuses and placing blame? In his book, *The Seven Habits of Highly Effective People*, Stephen R. Covey wrote, "Look at the word *responsibility*—(response-ability)—the ability to choose your response. Highly proactive people recognize that responsibility. They do not blame circumstances, conditions, or conditioning for their behavior. Their behavior is a product of their own conscious choices, based on values, rather than a product of their conditions, based on feeling."

When things go wrong, the responsible person asks, "What is it in *me* that caused this to happen?" "What did I fail to consider?" "What will I do differently next time?" In other words, the person who has accepted responsibility for his or her future says, **"If it is to be, it's up to me!"**

Kay James was born on the kitchen table of her family's apartment in Portsmouth, Virginia. Kay was born into poverty, raised in a public housing project, and discriminated against because she was black. She experienced a childhood that was filled with rejection and loneliness. She was mistreated by her alcoholic father, who later left the family and by her aunt, who she went to live with at the age of six. All the odds were against Kay. In fact, she was one of those babies that many people might say never should have been born. However, instead of blaming people and making excuses, Kay worked hard, practiced self-discipline, and took personal responsibility for her life. After graduating from high school, Kay went to college at Hampton Institute (now Hampton University) and graduated with a degree in history and secondary education. She took advantage of the opportunities that came her way. Kay went from the public-housing projects in Richmond, Virginia, to the corridors of power in Washington, D.C. Kay James served in the White House during the Bush Administration, and went on to serve as the Dean of Robertson School of Government at Regent University in Virginia Beach, Virginia.

Responsibility is defined by Webster's dictionary as "Having to account for one's actions: answerable, having a duty or obligation, being a source or cause, dependable."

Write down what it means to be responsible for:

Your future _____

_____

_____

_____

Choosing your own values _____

_____

_____

_____

Your choices and actions _____

_____

_____

_____

Your attitude _____

_____

_____

_____

Your abilities, gifts, and talents _____

_____

_____

_____

Your potential _____

_____

_____

_____

The achievement of your vision _____

_____

_____

_____

Your behavior with other people—parents, siblings, friends, students, and teach-
ers _____

_____

_____

_____

Your communication with others _____

_____

_____

Your schoolwork _____

_____

_____

_____

Your time _____

_____

_____

_____

Your own happiness _____

_____

_____

_____

Your own self-esteem _____

_____

_____

_____

Write down what it means to be responsible to society.

_____

_____

_____

_____

_____

_____

> *"It's not what happens to you... it's what you do about it."*
>
> **—W Mitchell**
> **Motivational speaker & author**

A FORMULA TO REMEMBER:
E + R = O

E - Stands for the *events* in your life.

R - Stands for your *response* to those events.

O - Stands for the *outcome* as a result of E + R.

It's not what happens to you that determines your success or failure in life: it's how *you respond* to what happens to you that makes all the difference. Everything in your life that you like or dislike is an *outcome* of some earlier *response* to a certain *event* that took place in your life. Therefore, if you don't like the outcome you have in your life, you must go back and change something in the formula. The only thing you have complete control over in the formula is *your response.* If you change your response, you will get a different outcome. Therefore, continue to change your responses until you get the outcome you desire.

RESPONSIBILITY WORKSHEET

Write down a current (or future) event in your life. Based on that event, write down your desired outcome. Finally, write down the response needed from you in order to achieve your desired outcome—*(See example below)*.

Event	Response	Outcome
Science class	Study hard and ask for help	An "A" for the semester

THE RESPONSIBILITY CREED

"I believe in the supreme worth of the individual and in his or her right to life, liberty, and the pursuit of happiness.

I believe that every right implies a responsibility; every opportunity an obligation; every possession a duty.

I believe that the law was made for people and not people for the law; that government is the servant of the people and not their master.

I believe in the dignity of labor, whether with head or hand; that the world owes no one a living but that it owes everyone an opportunity to make a living.

I believe that thrift is essential to well-ordered living and that economy is a prime requisite of a sound financial structure, whether in government, business, education or personal affairs.

I believe that truth and justice are fundamental to an enduring social order.

I believe in the sacredness of a promise; that a person's word should be as good as his or her bond; that character—not wealth, power, or position—is of supreme worth.

I believe that rendering useful service is the common duty of humankind and that only in the purifying fire of sacrifice is the dross of selfishness consumed and the greatness of the human soul set free.

I believe in an all-wise and all-loving God, and that an individual's highest fulfillment, greatest happiness, and widest usefulness are to be found in living in harmony with His will.

I believe that love is the greatest thing in the world; and that it alone can overcome hate; that right can and will triumph over might."

Adapted from a speech given by philanthropist John D. Rockefeller, Jr., on July 8, 1941.

RESPONSIBILITY ACTION STEPS

Write down a particular *outcome* that you have in your life that you are not happy with.

_____

_____

_____

_____

_____

Now, write down in detail how you **will** change your *response* **today** to get the outcome you desire.

_____

_____

_____

_____

_____

_____

_____

_____

RESPONSIBILITY
SESSION SUMMARY

- Responsibility is defined as "Having to account for one's action: answerable, having a duty or obligation, being a source or cause, dependable."

- Responsibility—"response-ability"—the ability to choose your response.

- The person who has accepted responsibility for his or her future says, "If it is to be, it's up to me!"

- It's not what happens to you that determines your success or failure in life, it's how you respond to what happens to you that makes all the difference.

- A formula to remember, E+R=O: Event + Response = Outcome.

REFLECTIONS

Use this page to write down any thoughts and takeaways that come to mind as you *"reflect"* on the session you've just completed.

_____

_____

_____

_____

_____

_____

_____

_____

_____

_____

_____

_____

_____

_____

_____

_____

_____

YES, YOU CAN!

"If thou canst believe,
all things are possible to him that believeth."

—St. Mark, 9:23

The "Y" in VICTORY stands for:
Yes, You Can!

No, it can't be done! Forget about it! You can't do it! Why don't you give up on that crazy idea and stop wasting your time? Are you going to fail ten-thousand times? Can't you see; it's impossible! That's what people said to a man by the name of Thomas A. Edison. And then one day, **the lights came on!** History is rich with the stories of "experts" who were convinced that the ideas, plans, and dreams of others could never be achieved. However, victory came to those who said, *"I can do it!"* Have you ever felt as if everything and everyone were against you? It's one of the loneliest feelings you will ever experience. And if you follow your heart's desire there may be times when you will feel that way. However, if you know that what you desire is right, you have faith in a power greater than yourself, and you possess the abilities and skills needed—you can say with confidence, **"I Can do it!"**

Wilma Rudolph was the twentieth of 22 children! She was born prematurely to Blanche and Ed Rudolph. At 4.5 pounds, this baby girl had a rough start. Wilma suffered from several childhood illnesses, including scarlet fever, whooping cough, double pneumonia, and measles. At age five, she contracted infantile paralysis caused by the poliovirus. As a result of having polio, Wilma was physically disabled for much of her early life. Due to the loss of strength in her left leg and foot, she wore a leg brace until she was 12. With the help of physical therapy, hard work, and perseverance, Wilma eventually overcame her disability. In high school, she excelled in basketball and track. It wasn't long before she started gaining acclaim for her running abilities. While still in high school, Wilma qualified for the 1956 Summer Olympic Games and won a bronze medal in the 400-meter relay. After graduating from high school, She enrolled in Tennessee State University and started training for the next Olympics. Wilma did not only qualify for the 1960 Olympics but also went on to win three gold medals and became the first American woman to do so in a single Olympics. Wilma Rudolph was considered the "Fastest woman on Earth." Her accomplishments are memorialized in various tributes, including numerous publications, documentary films, and a U.S. postage stamp.

YOU HAVE TO BELIEVE!

In his book, *You Can! Seven Principles for Winning in Life!*, Dr. Frank Minirth shares his motto: **"You can if you believe you can."** Belief is the knowledge that you're capable of accomplishing something. It's the conviction that you've got what it takes to live your dream. Belief is the inner voice that says, "Yes, You Can!"

Do you believe in your heart that you can live your dream?

Yes ❑ No ❑ I don't know ❑

Explain why _____

_____

_____

_____

What will be your source of strength when no one believes you can achieve your dream? (for example: your faith in a Higher Power)

_____

_____

_____

_____

What are you going to do when people laugh in disbelief at your ambitions? _____

_____

_____

_____

Write down the names of three people who you can count on to encourage you when you feel like quitting. (**Hint:** select individuals who are going after their own dreams. They will understand and be able to relate to what you are experiencing).

1. _____

2. _____

3. _____

Focusing on the reasons **_why_** you will live your dream will help you make it through the challenging and difficult times. Write down ten reasons **_why_** you will live your dream. (For example: "I will live my dream because I want to be an example of what's possible!")

1. _____

2. _____

3. _____

4. _____

5. _____

6. _____

7. _____

8. _____

9. _____

10. _____

YES, YOU CAN ACTION STEPS

Write down in detail *why* you believe you *will* achieve your goal.

_____

_____

_____

_____

_____

_____

_____

_____

_____

_____

_____

_____

_____

_____

_____

_____

_____

YES, YOU CAN SESSION SUMMARY

- Yes, You Can live your dreams!

- "If thou canst believe, all things are possible to him that believeth."

- Belief is the knowledge that you're capable of accomplishing something. It's the feeling that you've got what it takes. Belief is the inner voice that says, "Go for it!"

- Know where your strength comes from. It will keep you going when no one believes you can achieve your dream.

- Don't become discouraged when people laugh in disbelief at your ambitions.

- Create an encouragement group.

- Come up with enough reasons *why* you can live your dream, and you will.

REFLECTIONS

Use this page to write down any thoughts and takeaways that come to mind as you *"reflect"* on the section you've just completed.

_____

_____

_____

_____

_____

_____

_____

_____

_____

_____

_____

_____

_____

_____

_____

_____

CONCLUSION

CONGRATULATIONS! I am extremely proud of you, and you should be too. You have put in a lot of hard work. If you've made it this far, you've got what it takes to realize your full potential. You are the *one*. The *one* whom I was talking about in the introduction. The *one* who will do what it takes to succeed. I am certain that you will make it. I am ***expecting*** great things from you!

Pursuing your dreams will be difficult at times, but don't give up: "for in due season you shall reap, if you faint not." If you press your way through, you will actually be thankful for the hard times. Because it will be the difficult times that cause you to reach deep down inside yourself to find the strength to persevere.

The following story will serve as a source of encouragement to you. It will keep your hope alive in those times when you feel like giving up because it doesn't seem like you're making any progress.

In the Far East the people plant a tree called the Chinese Bamboo. During the first four years they water and fertilize the plant with seemingly little or no results. Then the fifth year they apply water and fertilizer again—and in five weeks' time the tree grows to ninety feet in height! Wow! Now, the obvious question is: "Did the Chinese Bamboo tree grow ninety feet in five weeks, or did it grow ninety feet in five years? The answer, of course, is five years, for if at any time during the five years had it not been cared for, it would have died.

Can you imagine working on your dream for a total of four years and seeing nothing for your effort? Many times your dreams may appear not to be succeeding. If you judge according to what you see (with your natural eyes) you may become discouraged. And if you are not careful you will be tempted to give up and quit trying. Instead, you need to "walk by faith and not by sight." That means continue the care and feeding of your dreams.

In order to live your dream, you must: Plant your dream with your *vision*. Care for your dream with *integrity*. Protect your dream with *courage*. Nurture your dream with loving *thoughts*. Water your dream with *opportunity*. Fertilize your dream with *responsibility*, and believe in your heart that *yes, you can!*

Best wishes 4 VICTORY!
Otis Williams

ACKNOWLEDGMENTS

I give thanks for everything that I am and everything that I hope to be to my Lord and Savior Jesus Christ.

I am grateful to the following individuals for their encouragement, help, input, and support; without them this book would not be a reality: Les Brown, Terence P. Calloway, Jim and Holly Canterucci, Judy Clark, Julie Clark, Jennifer Dailey, Omer and Renee Davis, Mary A. Dobbins, Michael and Lisa Dorsey, Don and Jennifer Ellis, Joe Hinson, Willie Jolley, George Jones, Leslie Kreines, Carol Lloyd, Greg Love, Rick L. Metzger, Daniel Miree, Jr., Kimya Moyo, Lisa M. Nack, Jim Pancero, Norman and Marie Payne, Lee Reading, Ernest and Stephanie Robinson, Robert Tuckman, Diana S. Williams, Gail L. Williams, LaShonda Williams, and everyone else who has urged me on to live my dream.

To my alma mater—Aiken Senior High School.

To Tom and Marilyn Clark who gave me an opportunity that changed my life.

To Pat Schmidt who believed in me when I did not believe in myself.

To the dedicated Steering Committee Members of the Cincinnati Youth Collaborative, who give their time, talent, and resources to make sure that our youth realize their full potential.

To Greg Walker who encouraged me to bring back VICTORY 4 Youth!

To Shanda Trofe and her team at Transcendent Publishing who helped me to breathe life back into VICTORY 4 Youth!

To Kennedy R. Williams and Kaleb B. Williams, my daughter and son, who are examples of VICTORY!

To Tanya Williams, my beautiful wife, who is a constant source of inspiration and who challenges me to keep moving forward.

Thank you!

ABOUT THE AUTHOR

Otis Williams is the founder and CEO of Otis Williams Limitless, a personal development company that teaches people how to train their fear so they can live free and share their gifts with the world. He is a highly sought-after award-winning speaker, facilitator, seminar leader, and personal growth coach. Otis has practiced—*and proven*—what he preaches. For over three decades, he has been educating, training, developing, and challenging people in the areas of motivation, change, leadership, and courage.

THE AUTHOR'S VICTORY STORY

Otis was adopted and raised in a low-income single-parent home. Growing up, he watched his mother as she refused to make excuses, accepted responsibility, and worked hard. It was his mother's example that made him say, *"If she can do it, I can do it!"* With a burning desire to have more than what the *"projects"* had to offer, Otis began studying and applying proven universal laws and timeless principles that govern success and achievement.

Shortly after graduating from high school, Otis joined the U.S. Army. While serving in the Army, he decided to face and conquer his fear of heights by jumping out of perfectly good airplanes and successfully completing the rigorous training to become an Airborne Paratrooper. In less than two years, using the laws and principles he was studying, Otis was promoted from a private to a noncommissioned officer.

As a lifelong learner, with an understanding of the value of both informal and formal education, Otis (a first-generation college graduate) earned his associate's degree while serving on active duty in the military, and both his bachelor's and master's degrees after re-entering civilian life.

After receiving an honorable discharge, Otis began a career in banking, with no previous banking or finance experience. By continuing to apply the laws and principles he had been studying, in less than 18 months, he was promoted from loan collector to assistant branch manager. Shortly after getting promoted, Otis decided to work on his communication and leadership skills by joining Toastmasters International.

After emerging victorious from among more than 10,000 speakers worldwide to capture the coveted title of **"World Champion of Public Speaking"** for Toastmasters International, Otis was convinced that, *"This stuff works!"* With a true passion to help people be, do, have, and give more, he founded the aforementioned **Otis Williams Limitless**, a personal development company that teaches people how to identify and use the proven universal laws and principles that govern success and achievement so they can live their dreams!